Monkey Business

Monkey Business

Heather Hammonds

Nelson
an International Thomson Publishing company I(T)P®

Melbourne • Albany, NY • Belmont, CA • Boston • Cincinnati • Johannesburg
London • Madrid • Mexico City • New York • Pacific Grove, CA
Scottsdale, AZ • Singapore • Tokyo • Toronto

Nelson ITP®
102 Dodds Street
South Melbourne 3205

Email nelsonitp@nelson.com.au
Website http://www.nelsonitp.com

Nelson ITP® *an International Thomson Publishing company*

First published in 2000
10 9 8 7 6 5 4 3 2 1
08 07 06 05 04 03 02 01 00
Copyright © Nelson ITP 2000

COPYRIGHT
Apart from fair dealing for the purposes of study, research, criticism or review, or as permitted under Part VB of the Copyright Act, no part of this book may be reproduced by any process without permission. Copyright owners may take legal action against a person who infringes on their copyright through unauthorised copying. Enquiries should be directed to the publisher.

National Library of Australia
Cataloguing-in-Publication data

Hammonds, Heather.
  Monkey Business.
  ISBN 017 0101 63 0.
  ISBN 017 0101 62 2 (set).
  I. Title. (Series: BlitzIt).
A823.3

Edited by Jill Lewis
Illustrated by Rupert Freeman
Cover designed by Christine Deering
Text designed by Christine Deering
Typeset in Clearface by J&M Typesetters
Printed in Singapore by Kin Keong Printing Co. Pte. Ltd

Nelson Australia Pty Limited ACN 058 280 149 (incorporated in Victoria) trading as Nelson ITP.

contents

Chapter 1 **The Birthday Present**   1

Chapter 2 **A Mischievous Monkey**   8

Chapter 3 **Rod's Bad Idea**   13

Chapter 4 **Monty Escapes**   20

Chapter 5 **The Banana Trap**   26

Chapter 6 **Trouble at the School**   32

Chapter 7 **Got Him!**   38

Chapter 8 **Safe Again...**   45

Chapter 1

The Birthday Present

"Happy birthday, Rod," said his mum and dad, handing him a small, colourfully wrapped package.

Rod had just had a big birthday party, with lots of food, games and a large ice-cream cake. Now it was over, and only his best friend, Sean, was still at his house. Rod's parents had made him wait until the party was finished before they gave him his present, so Rod knew that it must be something really special.

"Hurry up and open it," said Sean, who wanted to see what it was almost as much as his friend did.

At last Rod got the paper off and found that there were two presents, not just one.

"Computer games – great!" he exclaimed, examining the boxes. "Wow, 'Alien Monsters'. I saw this advertised on TV and it looked fantastic!"

"Glad you like it, son," said his father. "But remember to be careful when you use the computer. It's an expensive piece of equipment, not just a toy."

Rod's family had recently bought a brand new fancy computer, and his father was worried the kids might muck it up. It annoyed Rod at times, because he was sure he knew more about computers than his parents did. Anyway, if he did do anything wrong, good old Sean would be able to fix it, because he was a real whiz with computers.

"Look at this one, Rod," said Sean, picking up the other present as they wandered off to the study where Rod's parents kept the computer. "This might be fun, too."

On the front cover of the box was a picture of a cute little monkey wearing a pair of shorts and a T-shirt. Above the monkey, bold yellow letters read:

Monty the Marmoset – the screen saver and anti-virus program that children will love!

"What a load of rubbish," scoffed Rod. "Mum and Dad should have bought this for my little sister."

"Hold on a minute," said Sean. "I know it looks babyish, but it's not as bad as it seems. See – it's a good virus checker and you can get the monkey to do things, like pop up on the screen when you turn the computer on, and say your name."

"Well, don't tell my parents because I wouldn't want to hurt their feelings, but I don't think much of it. You can take it home tonight and try it out on your computer if you like," replied Rod. "I'm going to be too busy playing 'Alien Monsters', anyway."

For the next hour, Rod and Sean happily battled a whole army of horrible computer monsters, until it was time for Sean to go home.

"Great party, Rod – see you tomorrow at school," Sean called out as he waved goodbye to his friend.

Sean didn't feel much like his dinner that night after all the party food he'd eaten at Rod's house, but he stuffed a bit in his mouth to please his mum. He left the table as soon as he could and, taking Rod's unwanted present up to his room, he switched on his own computer.

Sean's computer wasn't a fancy new one like Rod's. His parents didn't have much money, and had only been able to buy him a second-hand one for Christmas. It was good enough to run a few older games though, and stuff like 'Monty the Marmoset', even if it was a bit slow sometimes. Monty's program came on one little computer disk, so Sean pushed it into the slot in his machine and carefully followed the instructions on the box explaining how to load it. It was easy, really.

In no time at all, a bright little cartoon monkey just like the one in the picture jumped up onto Sean's computer screen. He had a cute round face, with white tufty ears and an enormous long tail that waved about behind him.

"I am now ready for action," he said in a funny voice with a strange accent. "What do you want me to do first? Scan your computer for viruses? Do a little dance, perhaps? Type what you want on your computer keyboard."

"Gee," said Sean to himself. "Do a little dance? That's amazing! How can the monkey talk like that when his program only came off one single computer disk and is playing on my old computer?"

He carefully typed the words 'virus scan' on his keyboard and waited to see what would happen. The monkey pulled a face, turned around and walked off the edge of the screen with his hands on his hips, looking just like a person who was off to do a very hard job. Sean chuckled to himself as he waited for his computer to work. Rod didn't know what he was missing out on – this computer program must have cost his parents a fortune!

A few seconds later, Monty the Marmoset walked onto the screen again.

"Is that it?" he yelled. "Is that all the computer space I'm going to get to run around in? It's pathetic. You're not even connected to the Internet! What am I supposed to do all day? No – your computer doesn't have any viruses, but then, it's such a worn out old thing that no self-respecting virus would bother to infect it anyway!"

And with those words, Monty stomped back off the computer screen, leaving it blank.

Sean's mouth fell open in surprise.

"What's going on?" he whispered. "This can't be happening."

He rubbed his eyes hard and sat back in his chair. He told himself that he must be seeing things. Too many sweets and red cordial at Rod's party – that was it! Looking over at his bedroom mirror and poking his round stomach, Sean wondered if he'd been eating too much junk food lately. Perhaps it was time to cut down!

Shaking his head, he switched off his computer, packed Rod's computer disk back into its box and went in search of his mum.

"I'll have a look at it again later, when I feel a bit better," he promised himself.

Chapter 2

A Mischievous Monkey

Sean's mum said he looked tired, and bundled him off to bed, as it was a school day the next day. But although he tried hard, Sean couldn't go to sleep. He ended up staring at the shadows in the corner of his room, where his computer sat quietly on his desk. Had he been imagining things? It was a funny sort of thing to imagine though – Monty the Marmoset marching on and off the screen, saying words that he shouldn't be able to say.

Eventually, Sean gave up trying to sleep and got up. In the dark, he switched his computer back on. It gave a little beep and began to warm up – but there was something different about it. It was running much faster than usual and thousands of bright dots zipped across the screen. Instead of making the usual chiming noise when it was ready for use, a loud fanfare blasted from the speakers, giving Sean a fright. Finally, the screen turned a golden colour and the monkey walked out onto it.

"Hello again. I've forgiven you," Monty said in his funny voice. "It's probably not your fault that you've only got an old computer, but it's just my luck to get sold to you, instead of someone with a nice big one. Monkeys love to play tricks, you see, and on a small computer, I can't have much fun at all."

Sean smacked himself on the side of the head to make sure he wasn't dreaming. He wasn't.

"Well? Can you hear me? I'm trying my best to be nice to you. I've done you a favour and changed some of the programs in this computer so that they aren't as boring," said Monty.

"You're only a computer program, so how can you speak and act the way you do?" Sean asked nervously.

"I don't know," was the reply. "Who cares, anyway?"

"Well, I do, actually," said Sean. "And what have you done to my computer?"

He wondered if the 'Monty the Marmoset' program had been interfered with by some very clever computer programmer at the factory where it was made, as a joke. It was the only reason he could think of for the amazing behaviour of the monkey.

"I told you – I've jazzed it up a bit," replied Monty, crossing his long monkey arms and tapping his foot on what should have been the floor, if he hadn't been inside a computer. "Look – are we going to be friends, or what? You bought me, so now we're stuck with each other."

"Well, actually," said Sean. "I didn't buy you. You belong to a friend of mine but he let me try you out on my computer first, because he was busy with another game he was given called 'Alien Monsters'."

"What?" stormed Monty. "Oh great – that's just great. He prefers stupid war games to something as clever as me. What sort of a computer has he got? One from the 1970s?"

"No," replied Sean. "He has the latest model, and his dad has had it connected to the Internet as well."

With that, Monty the Marmoset actually began to look happy. He began to smile and he unfolded his arms, clapping his hands together.

"Fantastic! Just put me back on my disk and take me to him."

"How do I put you back on your disk?" asked Sean.

"Stick it in the computer and I'll do the rest, dummy."

Feeling as though he was in a dream, Sean took Monty's computer disk from its box and poked it in the slot again. The little monkey skipped from the screen and the disk whirred for a moment. Then all was silent.

"I suppose that's it," Sean thought to himself, taking the disk out. "Wait until Rod finds out about this. There is no way he is going to believe me!" Sean hardly believed it himself. Oh well, he would just have to go over to Rod's house after school tomorrow and show him...

Chapter 3

Rod's Bad Idea

The next day, Sean packed Monty's box in his bag and set off for school. He met up with Rod on the way.

"I'm so tired," yawned Rod. "I was up late last night playing 'Alien Monsters' with my dad. We were playing for so long that Mum told us off in the end."

"I was up late, too," said Sean.

"What – playing with that babyish 'Monty the Marmoset' I lent you?"

Sean looked across at Rod and wondered how he could explain what had happened. Rod was going to think he was nuts!

"It's pretty amazing," he muttered, looking down.

Rod burst out laughing.

"No, really," Sean insisted. "It's weird. I think that something was done to the computer disk at the factory. Some sort of clever trick. Wait until you see it!"

Rod stopped laughing and stared at his friend. He realised that Sean was serious.

"Okay," he said slowly. "What's so strange about it?"

"It's the monkey," replied Sean, knowing that he sounded crazy. "It says really funny things – as if it has a mind of its own. It has even done something to the programs in my computer! Look, you'll just have to see for yourself. I'll come around after school and show you, but we'll have to be careful the monkey doesn't do anything to your new computer, or your dad will get mad at us."

With that, Sean took Monty's box from his school bag and gave it to Rod.

"Don't tell anyone else about this until you've seen it," he added.

Rod was curious. He trusted Sean; they had been best friends for a long time and he knew that Sean wouldn't make up a story about such a thing. What had made him so excited? He was dying to know, and could hardly wait until after school. Then he had an idea.

Rod and Sean's school had quite a lot of new computers that the parent's club had raised money to buy the year before. Most of the computers were kept in a special room of their own, and they were all joined together into something that Sean and the teacher called a 'network'.

Students could use the computers in their lunch break, as long as they asked the teacher first. They were not allowed to bring their own games from home though, and would be banned from using the computers if caught doing so. But Rod was sure he could get away with sneaking 'Monty the Marmoset' on when the teacher who supervised the computer room wasn't looking. He wasn't going to wait all day to find out what Sean was on about! He kept his plan from Sean though, because he was sure his friend wouldn't want to risk being banned from the school's new computers. They were much better than the one Sean had at home. Rod didn't care though. He could always use his family's new one.

Classes dragged by for the boys that morning. Sean kept thinking about what he was going to show Rod after school and Rod kept thinking about how he was going to sneak his computer disk into the school's system. At last the lunchtime bell rang and most of the kids went outside into the sunshine.

Rod's Bad Idea

"Let's go to the computer room," Rod said to Sean, as they hung back.

Sean agreed, as Rod knew he would, so the boys went and asked permission from their teacher, Miss Foster.

"Are you sure you want to spend your lunchtime inside, on such a nice day as this?" asked Miss Foster, frowning.

The boys nodded.

"All right then," she agreed. "But don't take your lunch in there – eat it first."

The teacher knew that Sean was very good with computers, and she didn't want to discourage his interest.

Sean and Rod quickly ate their lunches and made their way up to the computer room. No other kids were in there – they were all out in the playground. There was not even a supervising teacher in the room.

"Why did you want to come in here today especially?" began Sean. "Oh, no – you're not thinking of putting 'Monty the Marmoset' on the school computers, are you?"

"Of course," snickered Rod. "There's nobody around to see us do it."

"Don't, Rod," said Sean in his most serious voice. "It's too risky. When I said there was something amazing about Monty, I really meant it. If we're not careful, he could cause an awful lot of trouble. You don't understand..."

"It's only a computer program," said Rod, beginning to get annoyed. "Anyone would think the monkey was alive, from the way you're carrying on. And if you're worried about getting caught by the teachers, and banned from using the computers, don't be. If we get caught (and we won't), I'll take the blame. It *is* my birthday present, after all. Not yours."

Sean didn't want to start an argument with Rod, who had a bit of a temper that sometimes got the better of him. Besides, they were best friends! He tried to tell himself that he must have imagined all the things that Monty the Marmoset had said and done the night before but, in his heart, he knew he hadn't.

What would the monkey do if he got loose in the school's big network system? What programs might he change? The network was connected to the Internet too, and to other schools...

Hopefully, Monty would behave himself.

Chapter 4

Monty Escapes

"Okay, here we go," said Rod, switching on one of the computers and pushing his disk into it.

Soon Monty appeared on the screen. This time he was dressed in a cool blue T-shirt and shorts, with a matching baseball cap. He still looked like a cartoon figure, but neither boy had ever seen a cartoon whose movements were so realistic. Sean was sure that Monty had also grown bigger since he'd seen him last, and his long tail was much bushier!

"Hello there," he cackled. "I'm Monty the Marmoset, the most handsome and clever creature you're ever likely to meet. Is this computer my new home? It had better be more modern than the last one I was put on! Perhaps I could do a virus scan?"

Rod roared with laughter.

"I see what you mean, Sean," he spluttered. "This is brilliant!"

"Don't ask him to search for computer viruses," whispered Sean. "He'll be away for ages if you do. This system is too big."

"Stop whispering amongst yourselves and tell me what you want me to do," yelled Monty impatiently, jumping up and down and pointing at Rod. "Are you the boy who owns me? This other kid said he would take me to you. I want to see your computer and I can't wait for you to tell me what to do, so see you later."

Rod stopped laughing.

"Wait a minute!" he called out urgently.

The monkey, who had been moving towards the edge of the screen, stopped and looked around at the boys.

"Well?" he asked. "What now?"

"This isn't my computer," Rod said. "I just put you in here to have a quick look at you. I don't want you to go anywhere, or do anything."

"Come back on to your disk and Rod will take you home to his own computer," said Sean in a persuasive voice. "He's got a much smarter computer than this one. It's brand new!"

Monty looked out of the screen at the boys and frowned.

"If this isn't your computer, whose is it?" he asked.

"My school's," blurted out Rod. "And it's a big one; you might get lost in there."

"Get lost?" cackled Monty. "No way! You forget, I'm a computer program – how could I get lost? I'm going to do a little bit of exploring."

"Sometimes you're an idiot, Rod," sighed Sean, as Monty disappeared from the screen. "I told you not to put him on the school computer and now look what has happened! He could get up to anything in there. After all, he is a monkey, and monkeys are always mischievous."

Rod took a minute to answer his friend. He sat in his chair, staring at the screen and trying to make sense of what he'd just seen.

"Sean, Monty the Marmoset can't be anything more than a very clever computer program. Like you said in the first place, it has probably been interfered with by some smart person at the factory where it was made. It shouldn't be able to actually *do* anything on its own. Maybe you noticed changes on your own computer at home because something was going wrong with it. Computers do break down now and again. We don't have anything to worry about, do we?"

Sean shrugged his shoulders. Whatever Rod said, he knew that Monty had definitely changed his own computer. There had been nothing unusual about it before he'd installed the new program. What had Rod done? A monkey loose in the school's brand new computer system – what terrible things might he do?

The boys waited for all of the rest of their lunch break, hoping that Monty the Marmoset would return to their computer screen. But he didn't bother to come back. At one stage, a teacher poked her head in the room, and Sean and Rod just pretended they were playing one of the school's maths games. When the bell rang to signal the end of lunchtime, they couldn't wait any longer – they had to go back to class. Rod took his computer disk out of the machine and stuck it in his pocket.

"I'll bet a year's pocket money that he isn't on that now," said Sean. "Try it on your computer when you get home and you'll see."

"Don't be silly," answered Rod in a grumpy voice. "Computer games don't come off your disk and leave it empty after you've put them on a computer. You know that."

But secretly, Rod knew that no matter how strange it seemed, his friend might be right.

Chapter 5

The Banana Trap

All through the rest of the school day, Sean worried. What was Monty the Marmoset up to? He and Rod would not be able to get another turn on the school's computers until the next morning when they had their class computer lesson. Would they find him on their screen then, or would he have run off down the school's telephone line to somewhere else in the world, on the Internet? And then how would they find him?

"We've got to try and get him out of there," he said to Rod, as they dawdled home from school.

"Let's see if we can load this disk into my computer first, before you start panicking," Rod replied. "I still think that it's just a trick and we'll find the monkey is still on it, like it would be if it was a normal computer program."

Sean shook his head and looked doubtful. He didn't hold out much hope.

When the boys got back to Rod's house, Rod's mum was home. She gave them something to drink and a piece of cake each.

While they were sitting at the kitchen table Rod asked, "Mum, where did you and Dad buy that screen saver and anti-virus program for me?"

Rod's mum looked puzzled. "I got it from the computer shop up the road, at the same time as your father bought 'Alien Monsters'. Why, is there something wrong with it?"

"Oh, no, Mum, it's great," said Rod quickly. "I just wondered, that's all."

Sean and Rod looked at each other. If Rod's mum only knew…

"It's no use. I told you he wouldn't be on there any more," sighed Sean, after the boys had spent half an hour trying to get the computer disk that used to have Monty on it to work. "He really has escaped into the school computer!"

"What are we going to do now?" groaned Rod. "That horrible computer monkey could do all sorts of things to the school's brand new computers. The parents' club saved up really hard for them last year and it would be terrible if Monty wrecked the computers."

"Well, he's rude and cheeky and he mucked around with my computer, but we don't know for sure that he actually wants to *wreck* anything," said Sean, trying his best to think of a way to get Monty back on his disk.

Then, suddenly, Sean had an idea.

"Rod," Sean grinned. "What do real live monkeys like more than anything else in the world?"

"How should I know?" replied Rod, wondering why Sean was asking such a question. "Bananas, maybe?"

"Yes!" said Sean. "Bananas. I wonder... I wonder if a computer monkey would like computer bananas just as much?"

"You've gone mad!" said Rod, staring at his friend. "This whole thing is crazy. If we told anyone else, they'd never believe us."

But Sean wasn't listening. He was busy thinking. Monkeys and bananas... Bananas and monkeys...

"Haven't you got a computer program with lots of different pictures on it?" Sean asked suddenly.

Rod nodded. "Yes, my sister and I use it for our school projects. It's called clip-art."

Sean chuckled to himself. He thought he just might have solved the problem of the runaway computer monkey.

"Could you put the clip-art program on, so we can look for a picture of some nice fat bananas?"

Rod finally began to see what Sean had in mind, and quickly found what they were looking for. In no time at all, his computer screen was filled with a bright picture of a great big bunch of bananas hanging from a branch.

"Excellent!" exclaimed Sean. "Now all we have to do is copy this picture onto a spare computer disk."

Rod and Sean copied the picture and then switched off the computer. Somehow, neither boy felt like playing games on it any more. It was bad enough having Monty the Marmoset take on a life of his own, but the thought of some of Rod's Alien Monsters doing the same thing was just too much for them. It would be quite a while before they played those sorts of games again.

Sean went home and tried not to think about what might happen the next day. He switched on his own computer and was relieved to see that the bright colours and the fanfare had gone. He carefully checked through all of his programs, and they all seemed to be normal. It looked as though any changes Monty had made had disappeared once he'd left the computer and returned to his disk. With luck, it would be the same if the mischievous monkey made any changes to the computers at school.

Sean hoped that his plan to trap Monty would work. Somehow, he and Rod just *had* to get Monty back on his disk!

Chapter 6

Trouble at the School

The next day was bright and sunny, and, as the boys walked to school, they hoped their teacher wouldn't cancel computer class and decide to have a sports lesson outside instead.

"If the teacher wants to go outside, I'm going to say I have a sore leg, and ask if I can go on the computers anyway," said Rod, as the two boys walked through the school gate. "She'll believe me, because she knows how much I usually love sport."

"That's okay for you, but I'm pretty sure you're going to need my help to catch Monty and put him safely back on his disk," sighed Sean. "It will need both of us for this plan to work, and she's not going to believe that we both have a sore leg."

The bell soon rang for school to start and, as it was Friday, Rod and Sean lined up in the main courtyard with all the other pupils. Every Friday their principal made a boring speech to the school that he had written before the assembly. The children and teachers had to stop themselves from yawning, stand up straight and pretend they were interested in what he was saying.

Usually the principal's speeches were full of stuff that would be in the school newsletter anyway, and also complaints, like how much rubbish the kids were dropping in the playground, or how noisy they'd been in class lately. But today, his speech was different.

"Boys and girls, teachers," he began, reading off a sheet of computer paper. "Before school starts today, I would like to say that I wish I was a red-bottomed baboon... What! Er, there seems... There's a mistake here..."

The rows of children in front of him began to shuffle about and a giggle or two was heard. Did the principal really wish he was a red-bottomed baboon? Some of the younger grades seemed to believe what he'd said.

The principal quickly looked through the rest of his speech and, as he did, his face became pink, then red, then a really dark purple.

"Who has been interfering with my computer, or printer?" the whole school heard him hiss to a teacher standing next to him. "My speech is full of rubbish!"

Rod and Sean sneaked a look at each other. The principal must have typed his speech on the computer in his office. The boys knew who had interfered with it. Monty! There were a few minutes of confusion amongst the teachers, and then the angry principal dismissed the school. Each class quietly headed to their room.

"Cross your fingers we get to do computer class first, before anything else happens," whispered Sean.

The boys were in luck. Before anyone sat down at their desks, Miss Foster had them make their way to the school computer room. When the whole class used the computers, there were only enough machines for one between two kids. Sometimes this was annoying, but today Rod and Sean were glad of the fact.

"Okay, everyone, this morning we are going to work on the maths game," said Miss Foster, once the class was seated. "I want to see each and every one of you studying hard. Computer class isn't just fun and games, you know."

"How boring," somebody whispered.

Each pair of kids pressed the right buttons on the keyboard in front of them, and the maths game came up on the screen. The object of the game was for the players to get as many questions right as they could and move up a level every time they played. It really was boring. Today though, somebody had changed it.

"What's this?" asked one pair of kids when some words appeared on their screen:

I'm sick of school work. I think Miss Foster is a grouchy old bat, and the principal really is a red-bottomed baboon in disguise.

The teacher walked over to see what they were talking about and thought that *they'd* typed the words into the computer.

"Right!" she shouted. "Up to the office this minute! That's very naughty of you."

Sean quickly took the computer disk with the bananas on it out of his pocket and poked it in the computer he and Rod were using.

"This had better work," he muttered, as much to Rod as to himself. "Are you ready with Monty's disk?"

Rod nodded, keeping one eye on the teacher as she strolled around the classroom checking on the students' work.

All of a sudden, a song started playing out of a computer at the back of the room. The two girls using it screamed.

"Hey, hey, we're the monkeys," the speakers squawked loudly.

"Girls," scolded Miss Foster. "What are you doing? Where did you get that song from? You're only supposed to be using the maths game at the moment."

"We're going to have to hurry, before he does something really terrible," whispered Rod, as Sean fiddled with their computer to get the picture of bananas to fill most of the screen.

"I know, but this is harder to do than I thought," Sean answered quietly.

Chapter 7

Got Him!

As they were busy trying to make their computers work, the whole class suddenly heard a loud noise out in the hallway. The principal and some of the teachers were standing in a group, shouting at each other. Miss Foster opened the classroom door and poked her head outside to see what was going on.

"Since you were the last one to use my computer, it must have been you!" everyone heard the principal yell. "First, you make me the laughing stock of the school by interfering with my speech, then you have the cheek to put a picture of a baboon up on my computer screen!"

"It wasn't me," argued Mr Herbert, the grade four teacher. "And it was very childish of *you* to print off a picture of a chimpanzee with my name underneath it!"

"And who altered my spelling sheets? When I printed them out, they were full of rude words!" cried Mrs Davis, the grade three teacher. "I'd handed them out to my class before I saw what was on them. Those children couldn't stop laughing at me! One boy said he already knew how to spell them all!"

Miss Foster quickly shut the classroom door again and tried to pretend nothing was happening.

"Don't worry, I've nearly done it," Sean whispered to Rod.

A minute later, he had the picture just how he wanted it, and then he typed in bold letters underneath it:

Free bananas for Monty the Marmoset, from his friends Rod and Sean.

"Let's hope he sees this and comes over before the teacher does," Rod said.

"Give me Monty's disk, now," said Sean urgently.

He poked it into the slot in the computer in place of the first disk and waited. The trap was set. Now all they had to do was hope that their naughty little monkey took the bait.

As the boys stared at the screen, a small head suddenly popped up on the edge of it.

"That's very nice of you kids, to get these for me. Do you like all the tricks I've been playing, to make school more interesting for you? Soon all the teachers will be so busy fighting with each other that you won't have to do any more school work."

"Oh, thank you very much," whispered Sean, hoping the teacher wouldn't hear him. "We don't know how you do all this stuff, but we think you're pretty amazing."

Luckily, Miss Foster was too busy trying to fix another computer that kept switching itself off, so she didn't hear them talking.

"It's easy for someone as clever as me, and I'm having a great time in here," boasted Monty, as he swung into full view, hanging from something that the boys couldn't see just to the side of the computer screen. "For my next trick, I'm going to make all the computers play a brand new game that I've invented. It stars me, of course, and it's *very* exciting!"

Somehow, Monty seemed to have grown even bigger. Also, his clothes were flashier: he was wearing a pair of black and gold striped shorts, with a beautiful golden jacket to match. The length of his tail was sprinkled with glitter, so that every time he moved, it seemed to twinkle. To the boys, Monty looked as though he was becoming more and more alive all the time!

"Mmmm, I'll just eat these bananas first," Monty said, as he hopped down onto the branch that held the bananas in the picture, and began to make chewing noises.

"Here we go," said Sean to Rod.

Sean slowly moved the computer mouse up to the top of the screen, while Monty was too busy munching bananas to notice. Then he pressed a button on the screen, telling the computer to 'save'.

At the same time, Rod pulled out a little plug on the back of their computer that connected it to all the others.

"Hey!" yelled Monty, so loudly that the teacher turned around. "That's not fair!"

In a second, he was gone from the screen, and all that was left to see was the picture of bananas, with a few little square shapes missing from one piece of fruit.

"What on earth are you boys doing? Where did that picture of bananas come from? My goodness, what is the matter with everyone today?" asked Miss Foster, rushing over. "Rod, why did you touch the cord at the back of the computer? You know that's not something you're allowed to do."

"I thought I saw smoke coming out of it," Rod said, saying the first thing that came into his mind.

"Well, that's it! Computer class is over for the day," said Miss Foster with a frown. "A technician will have to check the whole system. Too many things have been going wrong with it lately, and if smoke came out of the back of your computer it could be dangerous."

Rod and Sean thankfully switched off their computer, and Sean pocketed the disk containing Monty.

"We got him!" he said, smiling at Rod. "Monty is back where he belongs."

The boys returned to normal classes that day. Although they heard that a computer technician came to the school to see what he could fix, they knew he would find nothing wrong with the system because the naughty little monkey who'd caused all the trouble had gone.

Chapter 8

Safe Again...

"Well, now that Monty's safely back on his disk, what are you going to do with him?" asked Sean, as he and Rod walked home from school that afternoon.

"I don't know," replied Rod, shaking his head. "I suppose we could always destroy the disk, so he couldn't do anything naughty ever again, but I don't like the idea of doing that."

"No, neither do I," agreed Sean. "It would feel a bit like killing him. Even if he is only a very clever computer program, he seemed so… life-like. The last time we saw him, he looked so real that I almost expected him to jump right out of the computer and start running around the classroom!"

"He had some good ideas, even if they were naughty," chuckled Rod. "You've got to admit, it was fun to see the look on the principal's face when he realised that his weekly speech was full of gobbledegook. And did you hear those teachers arguing? I wonder who it was that could spell all the rude words on that spelling test?"

"You could send Monty back to the shop your mum got him from and say the disk was faulty, I suppose. But then someone might try him out and get into the same sort of trouble we did," said Sean, who was secretly rather scared at the idea of Monty ever getting loose again.

"I think I'll just hide the disk in a box of

old clothes I've got in the back of my wardrobe at home," Rod decided. "That way, nobody else will have to put up with Monty's tricks."

"But how could he have been so clever?" wondered Sean, who always liked to know everything about how things worked. "I don't think the smartest computer programmer in the world could have made something as good as Monty."

"Well, perhaps something went wrong in the factory when his disk was made," said Rod, thinking hard. "But the truth is, I suppose we'll never know. One little computer disk – it was almost magic, wasn't it?"

Sean nodded.

"One thing's for sure – from now on, I'm going to be very careful with any new games I get when I first start to play them. One Monty the Marmoset in the world is quite enough."

"Yes, me too," agreed Rod. "After I've hidden Monty's disk, do you want to come down to the park with me and kick a football around for a bit? We've spent so much time on computers lately that we could probably use the practice."

"Good idea," said Sean. "Let's go!"

• • •

A few weeks later, Rod's mum was giving his room a spring-clean. She stumbled across the box of old clothes that he had grown out of, right at the back of his wardrobe, and decided to give them to her sister. Some of Rod's cousins were younger than him, and would be able to wear them. She didn't notice the small computer disk at the bottom of the box, but Rod's cousins certainly would. They had a new computer too, and liked nothing better than to try out new games...

About the Author

Heather Hammonds lives with her family at the foot of the Dandenong Ranges, near Melbourne. She has written a number of stories about Rod and Sean and their wild adventures and, in her spare time, enjoys exploring the Internet and walking her dog.

BlitzIt

BlitzIt **is here! Once you've read one *BlitzIt* book, you'll want to read them all.**

Mystery ... adventure ... alien visitors ... weird science ... spooky happenings ... *BlitzIt* has something for everyone!

Set A:
Bargains from Outer Space
Birthday Surprise
Expiry Date
Hell-ectric Guitar
Monopillar
The Twins in the Trunk

Set B:
Monkey Business
School for Bad Kids
Sickle Moon Ghost
The Aitutaki Phantom
The Haunted Quilt
Thunder Box